"We can judge the heart of a man by his treatment of animals."

-Emmanuel Kant

The Shoemaker

by Chris Lensch

First published by Experience Early Learning Company
7243 Scotchwood Lane, Grawn, Michigan 49637 USA

Copyright © 2019 by Experience Early Learning Co.
Manufactured in No.8, Yin Li Street, Tian He District, Guangzhou, Guangdong, China
by Sun Fly Printing Limited
2rd Printing 12/2021

ISBN: 978-1-937954-61-1
Visit us at www.ExperienceEarlyLearning.com

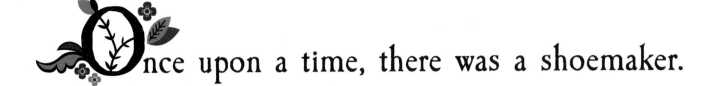

Once upon a time, there was a shoemaker.

He lived in the woods with his wife in a
small cottage.

Each day, the shoemaker went into his workshop to make shoes. And even though he loved making shoes, his workshop was quiet and lonely.

One snowy winter's evening, as the shoemaker worked, he noticed three mice huddled together outside his window.

They were shivering and cold, so the shoemaker emptied his only tool box, filled it with straw and placed the mice inside.

"This should keep you safe and warm," he told them gently. For the rest of the evening, he sat in his workshop humming and cutting leather with the sound of the mice scurrying about to keep him company.

When he was too tired to work anymore, he went off to bed. "I will finish these shoes in the morning," he decided.

The next morning, the shoemaker went into his workshop.

The shoes were finished! And they were beautiful!

"Someone has finished my work," the shoemaker said aloud. "And what a fine job they have done!"

He put on his warm hat, mittens and coat, and ran, as fast as he could, to the town market.

The shoemaker sold the shoes for more money than he had ever made before.

He bought materials to make more shoes.
He bought fancy foods and treats for himself and his wife.

Finally he bought some wood
and brightly colored paints.

When he arrived home, he told his wife the story. "Who finished the shoes?" she asked him.

"I do not know," he said, "but I have an idea."

The shoemaker placed the mice into an old wooden shoe.

With the wood he had purchased, he turned the toolbox into a cottage much like his own.

And with the paints, his wife made the cabin bright and happy.

They placed the mice into their new home
and fed them cheese and bread.

For the rest of the day, the shoemaker
sat in his workshop humming and cutting
leather with the mice scurrying about to
keep him company.

When he was too tired to work anymore,
he went off to bed.

The next morning, the shoemaker went into his workshop and once again there was a fine pair of shoes awaiting him.

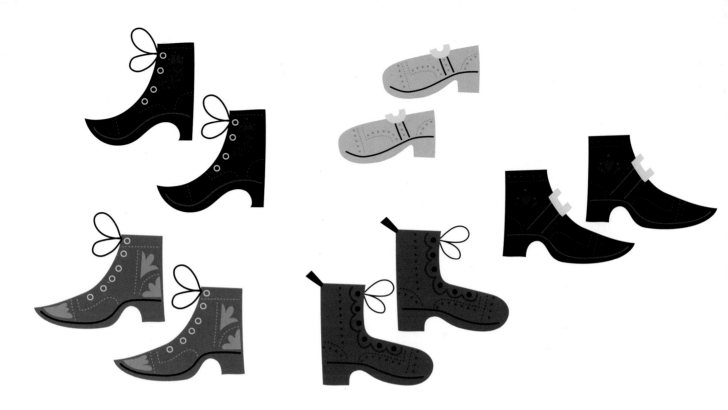

And so it went. Each day, the shoemaker sat in his workshop humming and cutting leather with the mice scurrying about to keep him company. Each morning, a fine pair of shoes was waiting for him.

The mice had a safe, warm place to live and the shoemaker's workshop never felt lonely again.